Play Foundations

Bugs and Animals

Liz Powlay

Acknowledgements

© 2008 Folens Limited, on behalf of the author.

United Kingdom: Folens Publishers, Waterslade House, Thame Road, Haddenham, Buckinghamshire HP17 8NT.

Email: Folens@folens.com

Ireland: Folens Publishers, Greenhills Road, Tallaght, Dublin 24.

Email: info@folens.ie

Commissioning editor: Zoë Nichols
Managing editor: Jane Morgan
Design and layout: Infuze Ltd
Cover design: Infuze Ltd

Editor: Jane Bishop
Illustrations: Cathy Hughes
Cover illustration: Cathy Hughes

With thanks to the following for their permission to use poems and extracts:

All Early learning goals and Aspects of learning quoted in this book are taken from *Practice Guidance for the Early Years Foundation Stage* (Department for Education and Skills) and are reproduced under the terms of the Click-Use Licence.

First published 2008 by Folens Limited.

Every effort has been made to contact copyright holders of material used in this publication. If any copyright holder has been overlooked, we should be pleased to make any necessary arrangements.

British Library Cataloguing in Publication Data. A catalogue record for this publication is available from the British Library.

ISBN 978-1-85008-334-4

Contents

Introduction

Who the book is for

This book forms part of the *Play Foundations* series which provides guidance for practitioners to set up quality play scenarios or activities with young children. It is written for all those working with three-, four- and five-year-old children in a variety of settings. Although many of the activities are written with nursery or school settings in mind, they can easily be adapted for childminders working with children in their homes. The book will be of particular interest to all those working within the Early Years Foundation Stage (EYFS) framework. It will also be useful for parents*.

Learning through play

The activities in this book are based on the EYFS principles:

- Each child is unique and is a competent learner from birth.
- Positive relationships ensure that children learn to be strong and independent.
- Enabling environments play a key role in extending learning and development.
- Learning and development takes many different forms and all areas are connected.

The focus of the activities is on child-initiated learning and the emphasis is on process rather than product. There are suggestions for using your guidance, your language and your support to promote the children's learning as they explore and play. Many of the activities can be enjoyed outside. Being outside has a positive impact on children's sense of well-being and can help all aspects of development.

How to use this book

The book is divided into five chapters, each focusing on a different group of bugs or animals, with each chapter demonstrating how a wide variety of activities can support all areas of children's learning and development.

The chapters are:

- Bugs – fluttering and flying
- Minibeasts – crawling and wriggling
- Pets' parade
- Out and about
- Dinosaurs.

The activities

Each chapter has six activities, each focusing on either one or two Areas of learning and development. The activities give a specific Early learning goal for each learning focus. Most of the activities are designed for small groups of around four to six children, but in cases where individuals require more support, it may be relevant to work with just one or two children.

Each activity is divided into the following sections:

- *Setting up* helps to plan *Enabling environments*, with ideas for how to set up the activity outlining the resources needed.
- *Getting started* describes how to organise the actual activity.

- *Let's talk!* provides ideas for talking with the children about their experiences. It includes questions that could be asked and how to differentiate language to suit the children's varying abilities. There are also suggestions for making the most of assessment opportunities.
- *Top tip* links into *A unique child* and *Positive relationships* with ideas for developing the whole child – their self-esteem, confidence, health, well-being, safety and relationships with adults and peers.
- The *Differentiation* section includes ideas for personalising the learning by adjusting each activity to make it easier for those children needing support or more challenging for others. This section will also be useful for planning inclusive activities for those children who have special or additional needs.
- *Further ideas* suggest ways of extending and enhancing learning and development opportunities, linked to the activity.
- Photocopiable activity sheets are provided in the book and they can also be printed from the CD-ROM. They are intended to enhance children's play or to create game scenarios.
- Every activity page includes a Claude Cat box, which lists relevant resources on the CD-ROM.

The importance of ICT

Nowadays, young children are becoming increasingly familiar with using ICT as part of their everyday experiences. Stories, rhymes and songs can be enjoyed through television and computer programs, and many early years settings have interactive whiteboard facilities. Children are surrounded by texts that combine images, sounds and words both on screen and paper and they need to learn to read images as well as print. The CD-ROM that accompanies this book provides opportunities for children to explore and become familiar with visual text, photographic and drawn still images, moving images, sound and colour.

Using the CD-ROM

The CD-ROM has been designed for children to use with adult support.

Claude Cat

Claude Cat gives instructions or asks questions which are designed to encourage children to verbalise their observations, ideas and understanding. This will help you to assess whether they need further support or challenge.

The main menu

This screen has the option to select a theme.

The theme menu

When the theme screen is displayed, you have the option of selecting different resources, for example, an interactive picture, story, rhyme or song, by clicking on the appropriate icon:

| Songs | Rhymes | Stories | Photocopiable activity sheets | Interactive pictures | Photos (some have sounds) | Film clips |

* Whenever the term 'parent' is used this is taken to include parents and/or the children's primary carers.

Planning chart

Use this chart to help with your planning. Each activity focuses on either one or two Area(s) of learning and development. These are highlighted by the stars shown on the chart. The Areas of learning and development are divided up into 'aspects' and the aspect(s) for each activity are also provided on the chart. On the activity pages you will also find an 'Early learning goal' objective for each activity.

The following key is used on the activity pages:

 PSED: Personal, social and emotional development

 CLL: Communication, language and literacy

PSRN: Problem solving, reasoning and numeracy

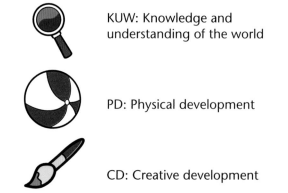 KUW: Knowledge and understanding of the world

PD: Physical development

CD: Creative development

Activities

Areas of learning and development

Bugs – fluttering and flying

Activity	Page	PSED	CLL	PSRN	KUW	PD	CD	Aspect of learning
Flying bug hunt	10				★			Time
		★						Dispositions and attitude
Flying ladybirds	12	★						Self-care
Dragonfly sculptures	13					★		Using equipment and materials
							★	Exploring media and materials
Bee patterns	14			★				Shape, space and measures
Butterfly wings	15		★					Handwriting
Ugly Bug Ball	16						★	Developing imagination and imaginative play
			★					Language for communication

Minibeasts – crawling and wriggling

Activity	Page	PSED	CLL	PSRN	KUW	PD	CD	Aspect of learning
Spiders' webs	18			★				Designing and making
							★	Being creative – responding to experiences, expressing and communicating ideas
Marching ants	19						★	Being creative – responding to experiences, expressing and communicating ideas
						★		Movement and space
Snails	20	★						Behaviour and self-control
Wriggly worms	21		★					Linking sounds and letters
What do caterpillars eat?	22					★		Health and bodily awareness
			★					Language for thinking
Tadpole pool	24			★				Numbers as labels and for counting

Assessment ideas

The EYFS centres on the development, care and learning needs of all children and planning to meet these individual needs, so children get the best possible start in life. Through ongoing observation we can decide where children are in their development and learning and establish their current interests and needs. These observations can then be used to plan appropriate experiences and identify any areas for concern.

Observation

Ongoing observation of children during their daily routines and play allows us to note their responses in different situations and to different people. Through written notes, for example on sticky notes, photos, video, things made by the children and information from parents we can build up a picture of each child and use this information to guide our current planning. Daily diaries, activity feedback sheets or tracking records can capture the children's progress over a longer period of time and at different times. These can be collated later by a key person and entered into the ongoing records for the child, summarising a child's achievements and development. There is no one 'right' method of observing; settings need to develop high quality methods of observation and assessments that suit the needs of their staff and the children and families concerned.

Planning

Planning is a process involving observing, analysing and reflecting on what we see and do with children, then using what we have found out to choose activities and resources and plan next steps in a child's learning. In this way we can personalise the children's learning and make the most of their strengths, interests and needs. Using the information from observation it becomes possible to see the stages individuals and groups of children have reached in their learning, development and interests and therefore to plan activities, opportunities and resources effectively. This might involve planning a specific activity to enable the child, or group of children, to extend their learning or further activities in order to reinforce learning.

Planning should include opportunities for the children to decide on activities they would like to do and be flexible enough for the unexpected that captures a child's imagination. Planning should ensure that children learn effectively with progression, through a wide range of interesting and varied activities. To aid planning the chapters in this book cover all the Areas of learning and development, with a mixture of adult-led and child-led activities, together with suggestions on how and what to observe and ideas for further activities.

Using your assessments

After observing the children, it is important to look at, analyse and review the findings, coming to informed decisions about each child's development and learning, highlighting the children's achievements or their need for further support. Parents should be involved as part of the ongoing observation and assessment process and information shared. Assessments should be used to inform planning for a child in both the short-term and long-term.

The 'Look, listen and note' approach of the EYFS is a helpful tool when deciding what to observe and how. On the next page this format has been applied to children learning about 'bugs and animals' giving some examples of the types of observations to make to help inform everyday planning. For each of the five chapter headings, there are ideas for what you should look out for especially.

Observation hints

Here are some suggestions to help you focus your observations and assessments when children are learning about 'bugs and animals'.

Chapter heading	Look, listen and note
Bugs – fluttering and flying	Observe how the children approach a task and the way they choose and obtain resources. How independent are they? Listen to how the children express their feelings about the garden area and suggestions for improving it. Make a note of children's physical skills as they tackle activities such as making models and decorating insects.
Minibeasts – crawling and wriggling	Note if the children give reasons and suggest expectations and boundaries when caring for animals. Make a note of the children's food choices, likes and dislikes at the setting and at home. Write down examples of mathematical language associated with counting, and one to one correspondence.
Pets' parade	Look at how each child uses independent writing for recording, communicating and labelling. Note if they can use creative and imaginative ideas to make models. Observe the skills children demonstrate while using ICT.
Out and about	Note the stories and poems the children return to and if they use the words and phrases in their play. Record the mathematical language children use when playing – positional, descriptions of shapes made, size. Listen to the sounds the children make to represent animals. Can they make up their own or do they copy others?
Dinosaurs	Observe how the children join in with group play and interact with others, sharing resources. Note the changes and patterns children see and comment on while making swamps and fossils. Observe how the children move – copying, spontaneously and the control they show.

CD-ROM resources

Find the bugs

Where are they hiding?

Early learning goals

Find out about past and present events in their own lives, and in those of their families and other people they know.

Continue to be interested, excited and motivated to learn.

Setting up

Select an area outdoors with some bugs, but few flying ones. Collect together magnifying pots, paintbrushes, camera, markers and laminated copies of the activity sheet 'Find the bugs'. Provide photos and books on encouraging flying insects into the garden. Obtain stones, logs, a container for water with a protective grid, water plants (tall mares tails, mini water lily), bug boxes, permanent plants to attract flying insects (buddleia, lavender, nettles, sedums, valerian), large planters and compost, if required.

Getting started

- Show small groups of children how to carefully search for creatures and lift them into the viewers using the paintbrushes. Explain how to use the activity sheet and make a mark for each creature found in the appropriate box.
- Encourage the children to explore the area and find different bugs, discussing and identifying what they find and taking photos. Look at the creatures, then let them go where they were found.
- Talk about wanting to encourage more bugs to come, especially flying ones and how they need shelter and food. Introduce the books, photos and interactive activity on the CD-ROM and encourage the children to find out what they could do to help. Using their suggestions, enhance the area together by planting plants and setting up habitats to encourage flying bugs. Record what you have set up with photos. Repeat the bug hunt regularly and compare what it was like originally with what is found on subsequent visits.
- Make a book in which to place the children's recordings, ideas and photos.

Let's talk!

Ask, *Do you know what your bug is?* For those needing more support look at it together and talk through its features. Note how accurate they are. Challenge children by asking them to explain how they found out what it was. Note how children use words to differentiate the past, present and future such as *last time*, *now* and *next* and how they describe changes they find. When looking at the books how do they describe the sequence of events and do they link it to their own experiences?

Top tip

Use the activity to introduce the idea that some plants and insects can hurt or harm us and that children must ask an adult before touching them. Invite parents and carers, especially fathers, to come in and help.

Differentiation

For those requiring support, amend the identification chart to show just the bugs present in your area. Challenge other children to devise a way of recording changes in the plants and types of bugs found.

Further ideas

- Plant annual seeds and watch them grow into plants for the area.

Find the bugs

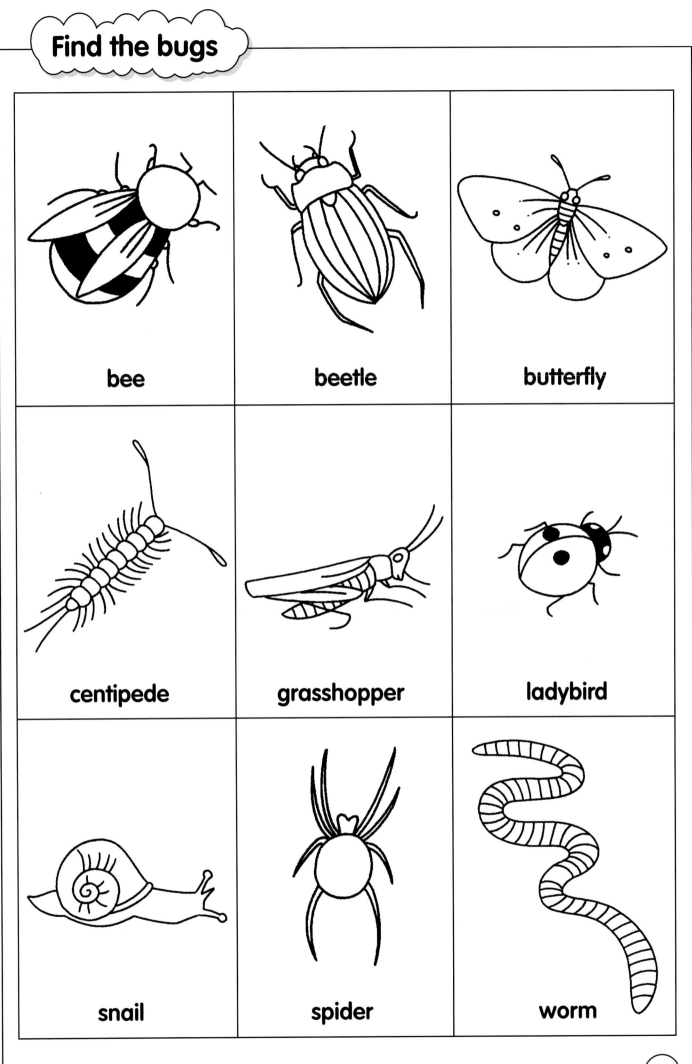

bee

beetle

butterfly

centipede

grasshopper

ladybird

snail

spider

worm

Flying ladybirds

CD-ROM resources

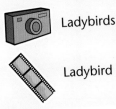

Ladybirds

Ladybird

Early learning goal

Select and use activities and resources independently.

Setting up

Collect together a wide range of materials in ladybird colours and shapes, for example paper plates and card circles, pipe cleaners, small pieces and circles of paper and fabric for spots, felt pens, red, yellow and black paint, paper, plastic and eva foam, brass paper fasteners, string, wool as well as scissors, glue and tape. Place in an easily accessible place in containers.

Getting started

- Introduce the topic of ladybirds to a group of children and share their thoughts and comments. Show the children the photo on the CD-ROM of the ladybirds and talk about their features such as colours, shapes, spots, feelers and number of legs. Explain that the coloured part of the ladybird is protecting their fragile wings and watch the film clip of the ladybird's wings coming out and it flying off.
- Invite the children to make their own ladybirds, encouraging them to select the materials they would like to use from the containers and work as independently as possible to make a unique ladybird.

Let's talk!

Ask, *What are you going to use to make the body?* Ask children requiring support, *How are you going to make the …?* Ask children requiring more challenge, *How are you going to join these together?* After finishing the ladybirds ask, *What does your ladybird have that a real ladybird has?* Watch how the children approach and manage the activity and their level of independence. Note those that are confident to suggest ideas and try them out on their own and those needing support. Observe how they select their materials: which children can decide on materials to use straight away with no support, which need some guidance, and which need to be given a suggestion?

Top tip

Recognise and praise each child's effort at the different stages, as well as the final ladybird so they develop a positive approach to 'having a go'. Be encouraging and supportive, giving help and ideas sensitively so that all the children make a ladybird.

Differentiation

For those requiring support, suggest a couple of ideas for the child to choose from such as starting with a paper plate for the body or cutting out a circle from foam or paper. Challenge children to devise a way of making their ladybird appear to fly.

Further ideas

- Display the ladybirds with captions celebrating what each child did well: 'Thomas cut his paper carefully to make the wings'.
- Share a story such as *The Very Lazy Ladybird* by Isobel Finn and Jack Tickle (Little Tiger Press). Paint, draw or make the ladybird in the story, with each child depicting it in their own way.

Dragonfly sculptures

Early learning goals

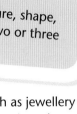

Handle tools, objects, construction and malleable materials safely and with increasing control.

Explore colour, texture, shape, form and space in two or three dimensions.

Setting up

Select photos and books with pictures of dragonflies and the ponds they visit. Collect together materials that could be used to make dragonflies and a pond setting: short lengths of very pliable wire, such as jewellery wire, cling film, dolly pegs, drinking straws, Cellophane, clay, play dough, card, paper, paint, glue, tape, glitter and place these on a table in containers.

Getting started

- Look at the dragonfly pictures together and talk about what the children can see: the colours, body shape, delicate wings and where they are.
- Invite the children to make their own pond scene complete with dragonflies. Show them some different ways of joining and using the materials safely, such as bending the wire to make shapes, scrunching cling film, wrapping materials around wire, curling and crumpling paper, bending and joining straws and making shapes from the dough and clay. Ask the children to suggest how these could be used to make the dragonfly body and wings and features in a pond such as rocks and reeds.
- Encourage the children to select the materials to make a dragonfly and pond.

Let's talk!

Talk about why we have to handle tools and materials carefully. *Why do we cut carefully? Why are short pieces of wire safer than long ones?* Introduce new vocabulary such as *bend, twist, pull, scrunch, poke*. Encourage the use of these words. Ask children requiring support, *What will you use to make the body?* For children requiring challenge, ask *How will you get it into the shape you want? What will you use to make the rocks? Pond? Wings?* Observe how confidently and safely the children use the tools and materials. Assess their level of competence and skill in manipulating them and whether they work in two and three dimensions.

Top tip

Help children to make progress in manageable steps by being aware of what they can do and then showing them appropriate new skills. Support them while trying these out, encouraging them to work together with peers and adults.

Differentiation

Provide help with bending, cutting and joining for those requiring support. Include some pre-made bodies and wings for the children to choose from in the materials provided. Challenge other children to make more than one dragonfly, using different materials in each.

Further ideas

- Look at the wings of the butterfly on the CD-ROM and compare them with a photo of a dragonfly's wings.
- Make a giant group dragonfly sculpture from a range of materials stuck into clay, such as twisted wire, straws, wooden dowel and twigs, securing dragonfly pictures to the ends.

Bee patterns

CD-ROM resources

Buzzy bees

Early learning goals

Talk about, recognise and recreate simple patterns.

LEARNING AND DEVELOPMENT

ENABLING ENVIRONMENTS

Setting up

Cut white card into strips 4cm deep and longer than the circumference of a child's head. Provide yellow and black paint and paper strips, pipe cleaners or card for antennae, brushes, sponges, scissors, glue and a stapler. Transform an outside area into a beehive with a sheet or fabric decorated to resemble a hive, draped over a child's dome tent. Make yellow and black stepping stones from thick cardboard, carpet or foam. Select pictures or photos of bees from books or the Internet.

Getting started

- Listen to the rhyme 'Buzzy bees' together and encourage the children to add actions to match the words.
- Look at the photos of the bees and the pattern of yellow and black stripes. Go outside on a bee hunt to look at the stripes and watch how bees move from flower to flower.
- Suggest the children become bees, making a striped headband to wear. Show them the resources and invite them to paint or glue paper to the cardboard. When dry staple to fit and add antennae.
- Invite the children to play outside, pretending to be bees flying to and from flowers and the hive. Introduce the stepping stones and encourage them to make a path to the hive, later developing the idea of making a pattern.

Let's talk!

Ask, *What are you going to paint on your headband?* Ask children requiring support, *What colour are you going to use first? What comes next?* For children needing a challenge, ask *What colours can you see on the bees? What pattern is it?* Observe to find out which children can make the pattern independently and those that need prompting 'what comes next?' Make a note of those children that need to hear the pattern said aloud as they paint.

A UNIQUE CHILD

POSITIVE RELATIONSHIPS

Top tip

Encourage the children to work together to make the path to the hive. Use the hive as a quiet place to relax after flying around as busy bees. Look at and taste different types of honey. Talk about how important bees are in the environment and if possible invite in a beekeeper.

Differentiation

For children needing support, say the pattern aloud as they paint, asking them to join in naming the colours. Challenge those confident at making black/yellow/black patterns with the stepping stones to try and make more complex ones such as black/black/yellow.

Further ideas

- Let the children act out the rhyme as they move along the black and yellow path.
- Make 'bee bread' spreading honey on bread and adding stripes with currants.

Butterfly wings

CD-ROM resources

Butterfly

Early learning goals

Use a pencil and hold it effectively to form recognisable letters, most of which are correctly formed.

LEARNING AND DEVELOPMENT

Setting up

ENABLING ENVIRONMENTS

Cover a table with a sheet of plastic and secure tightly with tape. Place ready-mix paint in bright colours, thin brushes, cotton buds, thin A4 paper cut into ovals, metallic marker pens and long fluffy pipe cleaners alongside.

Getting started

- Look at the photo of the butterfly on the CD-ROM together focusing on the circular patterns on each wing and the line patterns found near the edges. Make the patterns in the air, using fingers and whole arm movements, emphasising the anti-clockwise direction of the circular movements and the straightness of the lines.
- At the table show the children how to spread out a layer of paint on the plastic and draw small patterns in it with their finger, brush or cotton bud. Press the paper on top to make a print. When dry use the metallic markers to add circular and line patterns as seen on the peacock butterfly, again encouraging directionality.
- Make the patterns into butterflies by scrunching the paper together in the centre and securing with a pipe cleaner. Wrap it around the paper once to secure and then use the remainder to make a body.

Let's talk!

Ask, *Have you seen a butterfly? Did it have any patterns on its wings?* At the table ask children needing support, *What patterns are you going to make? Where will you start?* For children requiring a challenge ask, *What shapes can you see on this butterfly's wings? What patterns are there? Can you make them in the air? Which way do we go?* Listen to the children to note those that can describe the shape or pattern clearly. Notice those children that need reminding which direction to move in. Watch closely to see how much control each child has in their mark making and whether they have a preference for one type of mark. Note those children already using a correct movement independently.

A UNIQUE CHILD

Top tip

Make butterflies in pairs, placing a competent child with one less so. Invite the competent child to start making a pattern and invite the other child to copy them. Swap roles and make a second butterfly.

POSITIVE RELATIONSHIPS

Differentiation

For children learning to make correct shapes give hand over hand support after a chance to explore mark making on their own. For those competent at mark making and using anti-clockwise movement, introduce more complex patterns such as spirals, waves and zigzags.

Further ideas

- Draw butterflies in chalk on the ground for the children to paint over with water and brushes, watching them disappear.
- Make patterns with water in squeezy bottles on a path or wall.

Ugly Bug Ball

CD-ROM resources

Invitation to the Ugly Bug Ball

The Ugly Bug Ball

Early learning goals

Use their imagination in art and design, music, dance, imaginative and role-play and stories.

Sustain attentive listening, responding to what they have heard with relevant comments, questions or actions.

Setting up

Print off a copy of the party invitation for each child from the CD-ROM, or photocopy page 17, provide collage materials, scissors, glue and writing materials, fabric and crêpe paper to make costume parts such as wings and bodies, card for headbands and paint, fabric crayons and collage. Prepare a table for food and drinks (check for any food allergies or dietary requirements) such as ants on a log (raisins and cream cheese on toast), butterfly bread (bread and butter triangles sprinkled with sugar strands) and bee sticks (date and banana threaded on a straw). Set up an area outside with bunting, fairy lights, food table, rugs and play the song of the Ugly Bug Ball (original by Burl Ives or Disney version).

Getting started

- Listen to the story of 'The Ugly Bug Ball' on the CD-ROM. Encourage the children to think about what would make a good bug's ball. Ask them to think of a bug that they would like to be and how they could make a simple costume based on wings or body and a headband.
- Set a date for your ball and make invitations by asking the children to fill the gaps on the activity sheet to invite each other to the ball and then use colourful collage materials to decorate and fill the butterfly shapes.
- Make the food and drinks with small groups of children, dress up as bugs and go to the ball!

Let's talk!

Ask, *What would you like to do at a bugs' ball?* For children requiring support ask, *Which bug are you going to be?* For children requiring a challenge, ask *Can you remember what the bugs did in the story?* During the activities note who uses their imagination to think of ideas for the ball, their costume and invitation. Watch to see who takes on a role during the ball and joins in. Does anyone use ideas from the story?

Top tip

Encourage all the children to take part in the activities and ball, ensuring that no child dominates the others. Invite parents and carers to come in and help in the preparations and then send out invitations asking them to come to the ball.

Differentiation

Have some simple costumes ready to choose from and decorate for those children needing support. Challenge those who can think through their own ideas to design costumes for the adults and a programme for the ball.

Further ideas

- Make up party games to play such as 'put the wings on the bee'.

Invitation to the Ugly Bug Ball

To: _____

You are invited to our Ugly Bug Ball

On: _____

Love from: _____

CD-ROM resources

 Spider

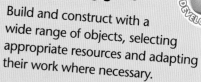

Early learning goals

Build and construct with a wide range of objects, selecting appropriate resources and adapting their work where necessary.

Express and communicate their ideas, thoughts and feelings by using a widening range of materials, suitable tools, imaginative and role-play, movement, designing and making, and a variety of songs and musical instruments.

Setting up

Place large sheets of paper, silver and white paint, marbles or small balls, shiny string, ribbon, silver thread, glue, glitter, scissors, pencils, Plasticine, sandpaper, card and fabrics in a box. Select a safe outdoor area where there are spiders' webs and a flat area to work. Print off a copy of the photo of the spider and its web from the CD-ROM, or display it on an interactive whiteboard.

Getting started

- Go outside and hunt for spiders' webs. Look in detail at their shape, size and colour. Notice if any spiders are around and look at them too. Compare the web and spiders with those in the photo and talk about their shape, size and colour.
- Show the children the materials and ask them to think how they might be used to make a web and spider. Demonstrate some simple techniques such as making holes safely with a pencil into Plasticine and threading shiny string through holes, dropping string into glue and glitter to make it sticky and rolling balls in paint and across paper to make lines.
- Ask the children to design and make their own web with a spider that dangles from it.

Let's talk!

While looking at webs ask, *How do you think the spider makes the web?* Ask children requiring support, *What do you like best about the web?* While making the webs guide children who require challenge by asking, *How are you going to make the web? How are you going to get the threads to stay in place? How will you stop the spider falling off the web?* While working with the children note which children are thinking about their design and modifying it if necessary and which have no plan or design and are randomly selecting materials.

Top tip

Praise the children's efforts and encourage them to try out different ideas, helping foster a positive attitude to trying out new skills and techniques and making mistakes and learning from them.

Differentiation

Discuss the shape and position of the threads of the web with children needing support and draw them together before making the web. Challenge children to make a spider that can move up and down on the web.

Further ideas

- Take photos of the finished designs. Print, laminate and display them in the area the webs were found.
- Read *The Very Busy Spider* by Eric Carle (Hamish Hamilton).

Marching ants

CD-ROM resources

 Ant

 The ants went marching

Respond in a variety of ways to what they see, hear, smell, touch and feel.

Move with control and coordination.

Setting up

ENABLING ENVIRONMENTS

Choose a simple non-fiction book on ants, or information from the Internet. Select the photo of the ant on the CD-ROM. Choose a piece of music to use when the children move like ants and a selection of musical instruments to represent the sounds of ants and rain. Provide materials for making instruments such as junk plastic bottles, tubes, containers, rice, beans, gravel and elastic bands.

Getting started

- Look at the photo together and talk about ants. Discuss their colour, shape, size and number of legs. Share the book to find out more information.
- In a large space, play the music and ask the children to pretend to be the ants, scuttling and scurrying around, carrying food and making tunnels. Introduce the song 'The ants went marching' on the CD-ROM, listen together and encourage the children to join in. Ask them to think of ways of making actions and noises such as tapping, clapping and clicking to resemble the ants and rain.
- Listen to the song again, this time ask the children to join in using the instruments and moving to the music.
- Ensure that the children can access the song independently. Provide the craft materials and encourage the children to make their own instruments to use when they listen to the song, decorating them to match the ants theme.

Let's talk!

Ask, *Have you seen ants? What were they doing?* Ask children requiring support, *Can you show me how ants would move?* Invite children needing a challenge to answer: *How would you move if it suddenly rained/you were carrying something heavy?* Ask, *Can you make a quiet sound with your fingers like ants scurrying?* Watch and note which children respond on their own, which wait and copy others and which remain watching. Note the levels of confidence and development each child has in the different types of activity and if they have a preference.

Top tip

A UNIQUE CHILD

Encourage all the children to join in, especially those less confident. Include those children who are happier watching by commenting on and asking them questions about what the others are doing.

Differentiation

POSITIVE RELATIONSHIPS

For children needing support, join in, working alongside the child making actions or movements for them to copy. Challenge other children to make and use their own instruments and make up an ant dance to the music.

Further ideas

- Set up an ant farm so the children can watch them safely close up.
- Cut brown paper to make an ant hill and draw on all the tunnels and rooms. Add thumbprint ants.

Snails

Early learning goals

Consider the consequences of their words and actions for themselves and others.

Setting up

Collect together equipment for a home for snails, such as a lidded clear tank, soil, stones, logs, food. Use the Internet and books to research information on their care. Print out pictures and add simple text so the children can access the information easily. Find a suitable safe outdoor area from which the children can collect snails. Provide disposable gloves to wear and a suitable container in which to carry the snails and where they can be kept for a short time.

Getting started

- Find out how to set up a home for the snails. Emphasise that this is for a short time and then the snails will be taken back to the area they came from. Place a clear tank containing moist soil, wood, stones and food in a cool place away from sun and heaters.
- Go outside on a snail hunt. Emphasise the need to collect them carefully so as not to hurt or damage them. Help the children think about, and put in place, expectations and boundaries for the care and observation of the snails and discuss why these are needed. Regularly check and care for the snails.

Let's talk!

Ask, *Where did you find your snails?* While observing ask children needing support, *Where do the snails like to go? What is their favourite food?* Ask children needing a challenge, *Can you find out how to keep them safe and healthy? Have we got everything we need? How can we make sure that they are looked after? Can we pick them up and play with them? Do we need to feed them? Why do we need to check them often?* Through talking and listening to the children, establish which children are already aware that we need to care for all living things and look after them carefully. Note which children can give reasons and suggest expectations and boundaries. Observe to see which children remain interested in the care of the snails.

Top tip

Help children understand that not everyone likes snails or wants to be near them and that these feelings must be treated with respect. Offer support to those who want to try and overcome these feelings.

Differentiation

Provide visual reminders of how to care for the snails for those needing support. Challenge other children to record their observations in their own ways.

Further ideas

- Look at a copy of the painting 'The snail' by Henri Matisse. Make a textured version, each child adding a piece of coloured fabric to a canvas base.
- Make enlarged photocopies of the snail from the 'Find the bugs' activity sheet on page 11. Use them to record the colourings and markings of different snails.

Wriggly worms

CD-ROM resources

♪ Wiggly Woo

Early learning goals

Link sounds to letters, naming and sounding the letters of the alphabet.

LEARNING AND DEVELOPMENT

Setting up

ENABLING ENVIRONMENTS

Print off a copy of the song 'Wiggly Woo' from the CD-ROM, enlarge it to A3 and display it at child height with highlighter pens nearby. Draw a large 'w' on paper or use a ready-made letter and display. Prepare an area for making and baking bread. Find a recipe for bread dough and gather together the ingredients or use a packet mix.

Getting started

- Listen to the song 'Wiggly Woo' on the CD-ROM and encourage the children to join in as they become familiar with it.
- Talk about *worm*, *wiggly* and *woo* all beginning with the phoneme 'w'. Invite the children to share, other 'w' words, such as *wet*, *waggle*, *warm* and *white*. Encourage the children to put the 'w' words into alliterative and silly sentences such as 'wet white worm'.
- Look at the large letter 'w' and draw it in the air and look at the copy of the rhyme and point out the letter 'w'. Invite the children to find the 'w' letters on the A3 sheet and highlight them.
- Next, make the bread dough and share it out. Explore ideas on how to make things with the dough starting with a sausage shape or joining small pieces together. Use most of the dough to make a 'w' shape and with the remainder make a 'Wiggly Woo' worm for the top. Bake and eat! (Check for any food allergies.)

Let's talk!

Ask children requiring support, *Can you hear the sound that worm, wiggly and woo begin with?* Ask children requiring a challenge, *How many other words can you think of that start with w? Can you put the w words into a sentence?* Ask the children how they will make their dough into a 'w' shape. Note which children can hear the 'w' phoneme at the start of the words. Listen to the children talking to find out who can suggest other 'w' words. Observe the children to see who can recognise and make 'w' when shaping the dough.

Top tip

A UNIQUE CHILD

If children in the group are unable to eat bread due to allergies or dietary needs adapt the activity to use a gluten free mix, or alternatively clay or other malleable material such as soap flakes modelling 'snow'.

Differentiation

POSITIVE RELATIONSHIPS

For children needing support, draw 'w' shapes on baking paper for them to cover with their dough. Challenge children to make other things starting with 'w' to decorate their bread such as a wand or web.

Further ideas

- Dig for worms in the garden.
- Draw giant 'w' shapes on the ground for children to wriggle, run, jump and hop along.

What do caterpillars eat?

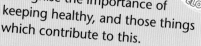

CD-ROM resources

 Caterpillar pizza

Caterpillar

 Early learning goals

Recognise the importance of keeping healthy, and those things which contribute to this.

Use talk to organise, sequence and clarify thinking, ideas, feelings and events.

Setting up

Collect together a copy of *The Very Hungry Caterpillar* by Eric Carle (Picture Puffin), the fruit mentioned in the story, the photo of a caterpillar printed from the CD-ROM, the baking equipment and ingredients from the 'Caterpillar pizza' activity sheet on page 23. Make cards showing the foods the caterpillar eats and one of the caterpillar with a tummy ache. Display an A3 copy of the activity sheet in the cooking area. Check for allergies and dietary requirements.

Getting started

- Read the story together. Explain that the caterpillar eats a mixture of healthy foods and others that should be eaten occasionally or as a treat.
- Invite the children to sort the pictures of the foods. Place those that are healthy next to the photo of the caterpillar and the others with the 'tummy ache' caterpillar. Ask questions to establish that the fruit is the healthy group and taste the fruit from the story together.
- Invite the children to make a caterpillar pizza. Ask the children to look at the picture recipe and say what is happening in each picture. Next follow the recipe together, asking them to say what they will do next as they make and shape their dough into segments. Place on baking paper.
- Decorate the caterpillar with the fruit before baking in the oven.

Let's talk!

Talk simply about how fruit, vegetables and healthy food keep you well and help you grow. For children requiring more support ask them to find the food as you name and describe its shape and colour and say which caterpillar to give it to. Extend children's thinking by asking *Which foods will help you stay well and grow?* Listen carefully to the children's responses building up a picture of what they eat at home, enjoy, dislike and if they know which foods are healthy and which a treat and should be eaten occasionally. Note what they eat at snack and meal times.

Top tip

Present the fruits regularly, encouraging children to choose them as a healthy snack. Be sensitive to each child's needs and feelings regarding what they eat, and respond appropriately when encouraging them to sample and eat new, healthy foods.

Differentiation

Break the session into shorter sessions for children requiring more support, and consider using a scone mix. Challenge children to form the caterpillar and decorate it independently. Invite them to sequence the pictures on the activity sheet.

Further ideas

- Read *Oliver's Fruit Salad* by Vivian French (Orchard Books) and make fruit salad.

Caterpillar pizza

You will need:

500g self raising flour
150g margarine
50g soft brown sugar
about 200ml milk
apple sauce
apples, pears, plums, strawberries, oranges, angelica

Sieve the flour into a bowl and rub in the margarine. Stir in the sugar.

Stir in the milk and make a soft dough.

Pat or roll out the dough to 1cm thick. Cut out circles and use to make a caterpillar.

Put the fruit on the caterpillar. Bake at 220°C/ gas mark 7 for 15 minutes.

Tadpole pool

Early learning goals

Count reliably up to ten everyday objects.

Setting up

In a shallow water tray, place stones of different sizes. Make water lilies from laminated pictures or plastic and number them from 1 to 10. Cut out tadpole shapes from small bubble wrap so the head is around 3cm in diameter and the tail 5cm long, glue on to plastic and add googly eyes. With a permanent marker draw spots on the bubbles of some of the tadpoles, from 1 to 10. Leave some blank. Make up a simple rhyme about ten small tadpoles swimming in a pond to a familiar tune such as 'Ten green bottles'.

Getting started

- Watch the film clip of tadpoles swimming in a pool and sing the simple rhyme, adding actions using fingers as tadpoles.
- Introduce the water tray and invite the children to play with the resources, making up their own games. Remind the children of the rhyme and invite them to act it out in the water tray. Place a water lily in the tray and ask the children to make sure the correct number of tadpoles are in the water.
- Play the tadpole game by printing off the activity page on the CD-ROM or photocopying page 25. Make a dice with numbers 1, 2, and 3 each marked twice and use tadpole counters (coloured pipe cleaner pieces with googly eyes). Help the children to take turns to roll the dice and count the number of spaces to move around the board game from the start to the home lily pad.

Let's talk!

As the children play the game ask those requiring support, *What number have you rolled? How many spaces can you move?* Ask children requiring a challenge, *What number is written on this lily pad? Can you find a tadpole with the same number of spots?* As the children play listen for those that use numbers names and language. Note if they can say numbers in order and if they count one to one. Note the number of objects such as stones they can count to and how many tadpoles or lily pads they can count out accurately.

Top tip

For children with English as an additional language and speech and language delay, think about different ways for the children to communicate their counting, such as showing fingers, drawing, using plastic counters, plastic numerals or dual language cards.

Differentiation

For children needing support, use numbers to two or three, as appropriate, in the water tray. Start the rhyme with five tadpoles. Introduce the numeral zero to challenge children.

Further ideas

- Make a collage number book with a different number of tadpoles in a pool on each page.

Tadpole board game

CD-ROM resources

Pet shop

Setting up

If possible, organise a visit to a pet shop. Collect together items for a pet shop in a basket such as soft toy pets, carriers, food, pet bowls, baskets, collars, leads, toys, blankets, beds, signs, till and money. Provide paper, card and writing materials.

Getting started

- Visit a pet shop and play the interactive picture on the CD-ROM together. Point out the features of a pet shop: animals for sale, items on the shelves, signs, till and baskets and trolleys.
- Show the children the pet shop in a basket. Leave the children to choose a place to set up their own pet shop and play with it. Observe how the children play. Return and compare what different children bought for their pets.
- Suggest some special offers such as 'Buy one get one free', 'Five items for 10p' or 'Everything 1p today'. Take on a role and write a shopping list. Invite the children to make signs for the special offers and help them try some of the offers.
- Introduce appropriate mathematical language as the children play.

Let's talk!

Ask, *What did you buy? How many things did you buy?* For children requiring support ask, *Who bought the most things?* For children requiring a challenge ask, *Which special offer is the best? If everything is 1p, how much will these two items cost altogether?* Note which children are using words such as *more, less, altogether, same, too many, take some away.* Do these link to the strategies they use, such as counting aloud, using their fingers, lining items up and adding to or taking some away. Watch to see which children choose to write independently.

Top tip

Joining in the play will help develop a caring and trusting relationship with the children. Invite parents to bring the family pet in and talk about where they got it from and what they buy for it.

Differentiation

Spend time playing with children needing support, taking on a role such as the shop assistant and introducing the vocabulary as you play. Challenge children to take turns to be shop assistant and make up an irresistible offer for the customer.

Further ideas

- Read *The Great Pet Sale* by Mick Inkpen (Hodder Children's Books), the story where 'everything must go'.

Pebble pets

CD-ROM resources

At the vet's

Early learning goals

Explore colour, texture, shape, form and space in two or three dimensions.

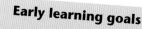

Setting up

Choose an outdoor area with large stones to collect or hide cobbles/stones (available at a garden centre/DIY store) outside. Provide a paper bag for each child and materials to decorate the stones such as fabric, papers, glitter, ribbon, foil, googly eyes, paint, markers and glue and scissors. Select the story 'Bonting' by Shirley Hughes about a boy with a special stone, in *The Big Alfie Out of Doors Storybook* (Red Fox).

Getting started

- Share the story with the children and talk about special objects or toys the children have.
- Invite the children to go outside and hunt for their own 'bonting'. Give each child a bag to collect any other natural treasure they find.
- Spread out the natural and provided materials, and encourage the children to explore them. Introduce ideas related to how they feel, look at the colours and introduce words to describe them such as *smooth, rough, shiny, crumpled.* Invite the children to each turn a stone into a special pebble pet.
- Place the pets in a special place so the children can return to them and add extra materials, if they wish.

Let's talk!

Ask, *Have you a special item or toy you would hate to lose? If you had a 'bonting' of your own what could you do with it?* Ask children requiring support, *What do you like about your stone? How are you going to decorate it? What are you going to call your pebble pet?* Ask children requiring a challenge, *Why did you choose to put this on your stone?* Look at the range of materials the children use, whether it is just one or two or a wide variety and how colour and texture have been considered. Note down comments children make when initially exploring the materials and explaining why they made their choices.

Top tip

Show children that you recognise they can feel more secure when they have a special toy by talking about them together. Ask them to bring in a photo to show their peers and make a display of these. Encourage parents and practitioners to add photos of special toys they had when they were young.

Differentiation

For children needing more support, encourage them to get started by suggesting they choose something they like the colour or feel of. Invite other children to make a home for their pet.

Further ideas

- Make up stories about the pebble pets and record them for the children to listen to.
- Photocopy the 'At the vet's' activity sheet on page 31 (or print from the CD-ROM). Cut out and fill in signs such as 'My name is …' and place with the pebble pets.

Home for a pet

CD-ROM resources

✏️ Take care of my pet

 Pets feel lonely too

🎞 Boy and dog

Setting up

ENABLING ENVIRONMENTS

Choose a soft toy as a pet for the children to look after for a week, and have an adult collect the pet after a week and answer the children's questions. Print the activity sheet from the CD-ROM or photocopy it from page 29, filling in the details to suit your pet. Provide a pet carrier and materials for making beds and toys.

Getting started

- Introduce the pet in a carrier and read the letter. Hold a circle time and pass the pet around inviting the children to stroke it, and to say something to it, expressing their feelings or offering suggestions about how to look after it.
- Listen to the rhyme on the CD-ROM and talk about how a pet needs to be loved and cared for. Invite children who have a pet to talk about how they care for them. Set up an area for the children to care for the pet and make beds and toys for it, as suggested in the letter. Encourage them to use these items in their play.
- When the owner returns, invite the children to talk about how they looked after the pet and how they feel about saying goodbye. Offer to have the pet back to retain the link for the children.

Let's talk!

Ask, *How can we look after the pet?* Ask children requiring support, *What would you like to make for it?* Ask children requiring a challenge, *Why might the pet have been left?* Note those who are hesitant about joining in at circle time, those who are sharing information linked to home and community and those who can show an awareness of how others are feeling.

Top tip

A UNIQUE CHILD

Be prepared for children who have had to deal with a difficult or stressful situation with an animal such as being bitten or losing their pet. Help children to gain the confidence to express their feelings by showing that you will listen.

POSITIVE RELATIONSHIPS

Differentiation

Support children who find it harder to express their feelings by talking together or with one other child. In a small group, challenge children to take turns to pretend to be the pet's owner while others ask them questions.

Further ideas

- Watch the film clip on the CD-ROM together and talk about playing with pets and safety near water.

Take care of my pet

Dear children

Inside this box is my _____ . I have had to go away and I hope that you will look after _____ until I come back in _____ weeks.

She is _____ years old and likes to eat _____ and drink _____ .

Please make _____ a cosy bed to sleep in and play with _____ each day. Can you make _____ some toys too?

I will see you all soon. Thank you for looking after my _____ .

Love from _____

Vets on call

CD-ROM resources

At the vet's

The injured pet

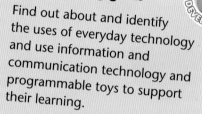

Early learning goals

Find out about and identify the uses of everyday technology and use information and communication technology and programmable toys to support their learning.

Use their imagination in art and design, music, dance, imaginative and role-play and stories.

Setting up

Set up a role-play area as a vet's surgery, include torches, walkie-talkies, telephones, computer (for appointments/slide show), a remote control jeep with trailer and vet doll, small toy animals to fit in the trailer, and medical equipment. Choose books based on vets, find pictures of pets, animals and vets on the Internet and make them into a slide show.

Getting started

- Listen to the story of the injured dog on the CD-ROM. Invite children to recount visits they have made to the vet with animals and inspire them by sharing the books.

- Take the children to the role-play area and show them the resources. Demonstrate how to make appointments and use the jeep to bring injured pets to the surgery. Provide enlarged copies of the activity sheet, printed from the CD-ROM or photocopied from page 31, for the children to use in their play. Encourage the children to place some of the animals and telephones outside on 'farms' or at 'houses'. Leave them to play and develop their own games.

- Introduce the slide show of pictures and demonstrate how to change them. Encourage the children to use these images to get new ideas for their play.

Let's talk!

Ask, *What happens at the vet's? Which animals did the jeep collect? Which photos did you like?* Ask children requiring support, *Can I see the animals you treated today?* Invite children requiring more of a challenge to tell you what they did to make them better. Watch the children to see which forms of technology the children prefer and whether they can work both simple equipment like torches and those needing more control such as the jeep and computer. Listen to see if a storyline develops as the children play and note who plays alongside and plays as part of a group.

Top tip

Help children to develop positive relationships by encouraging them to take turns and share the equipment and swap roles. Talk to parents about how to develop their child's ICT skills by letting them press the crossing control, start the washing machine or use the remote control.

Differentiation

Play with children needing support with new technology. Challenge others to use a paint program to design a poster for the vet's.

Further ideas

- Use a digital camera to take photos of each other playing and make a display.
- Watch a pet DVD or video and ask the children to select *play* and *stop* on the remote control.

At the vet's

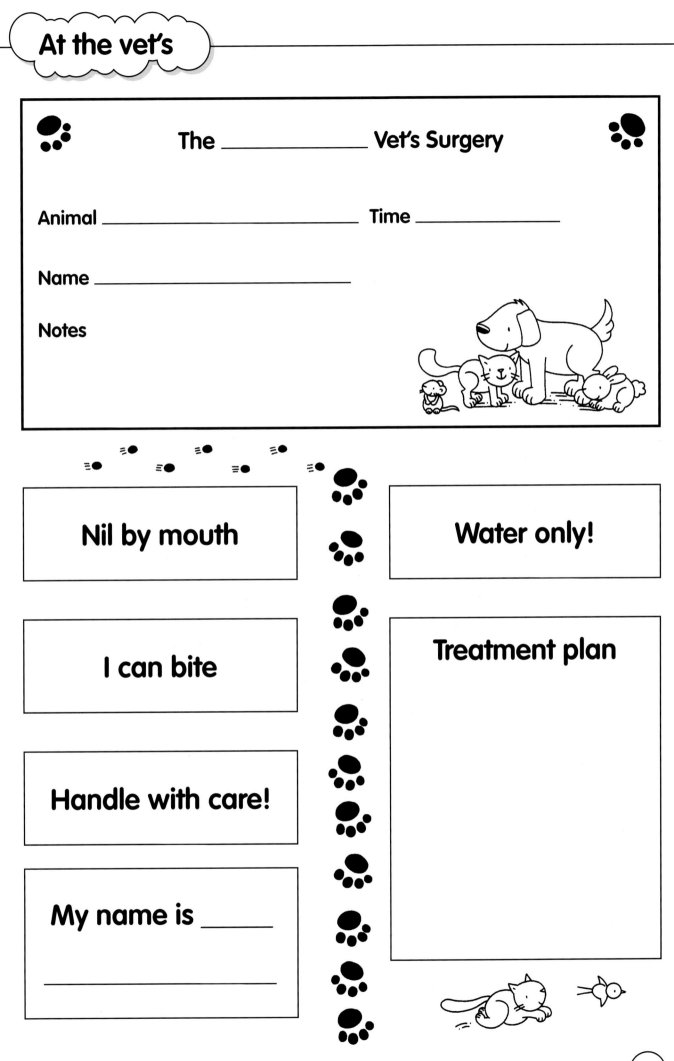

The _____ Vet's Surgery

Animal _____ Time _____

Name _____

Notes

Nil by mouth

Water only!

I can bite

Treatment plan

Handle with care!

My name is _____
_____

Rainbow fishes

Early learning goals
 Use a range of small and large equipment.

Setting up

If possible display a tank of tropical fish. Collect together different absorbent white paper such as thick kitchen roll, coffee filters and cartridge, laminating materials, sticks, thin ribbon, tape and scissors. Cut out one large fish shape and draw different simple fish shapes on the white paper. Place coloured inks, food colourings and powder paint in a tray together, provide plastic droppers, tea strainers and clean trigger spray bottles filled with water and aprons.

Getting started

- Look at the colours and patterns on the tropical fish in the tank and on the photo on the CD-ROM.
- Listen to the story on the CD-ROM. Listen to the story again and invite different children to find the colours as they are mentioned and place some on the large paper fish using droppers for liquid colours or shaking a little powder on using the tea strainer. Spray with water and watch what happens to the colours. Leave to dry and laminate.
- Invite the children to cut out fish shapes and experiment with making their own rainbow fishes using the colours and water. When dry laminate. Invite the children to turn them into stick puppets or hang them from the large fish to make a mobile.

Let's talk!

Ask, *What colours can you see on the fish? Why are rainbows so special? What sort of pattern are your inks making?* Ask children requiring support, *Which colours are you using?* Ask children requiring a challenge, *What happens if you use ink and then powder paint on top?* Watch how the children handle the equipment and note those that have difficulty using scissors, droppers or spray bottles.

Top tip

Explain to the children that they must only spray the paper and not the area around them or each other and help them to understand why there needs to be this rule. Teach the children the skills needed to use scissors, droppers and sprayers when they are ready to handle the equipment safely and with success.

Differentiation

Provide hand over hand help for those children needing extra support cutting, squeezing droppers and spraying. Challenge children to develop greater control by making a fish with spots, spirals and stripes.

Further ideas

- Make mosaic-style fish by printing with large sponges or tiny cotton buds.
- Place footballs in sea-coloured paint and roll them across large sheets to make a background for a fish display.

A hat with a cat

CD-ROM resources

Pet shop

Early learning goals

Use their phonic knowledge to write simple regular words and make phonetically plausible attempts at more complex words.

LEARNING AND DEVELOPMENT

Setting up

Collect together paper, pen, whiteboard markers, a range of hats and small toy cats. Stick pictures of items that end in 'at', such as a bat, mat, hat, fat and cat on card, leaving space to write the word, and laminate. Make a set for items that do not end in 'at' such as pan, bed, dog. Place a cat in some of the hats and leave others empty. Find a story based on rhymes using the 'at' ending such as *Pat the Cat* by Colin and Jacqui Hawkins (Pat and Pals Limited).

Getting started

• Share the story with the children. Try to remember all the 'at' words together and check back in the book. Ask the children to help you write the words, encouraging them to say the phonemes they hear.
• Show the children the hats and cards with pictures. Tell them that hidden inside some of the hats are cats. Explain that if they find a cat then they can choose a picture that has the 'at' sound to put in the hat. If there is no cat they choose any other picture.
• Leave the children to explore the hats and choose the pictures, observing how they get on. Return and suggest that they pull out a card and try to write the word under the picture.

Let's talk!

Ask, *What did you notice about that story? Cat, Pat, mat … what phonemes do they all have?* Ask children requiring support, *Have you found a cat in there? Which card are you going to pop inside?* Ask children requiring more challenge, *If we wanted to write cat what phonemes would we write?* Note the phonemes the children hear and say and if they are in the correct order. Watch as the children write to see which phonemes they can write independently and note which they need help with.

Top tip

Ask the children to take responsibility for getting the game ready for the next group, collecting together the cards and hiding the cats. Make up a story bag containing the book and game for children to take home and share with their families.

Differentiation

Support children by asking them what sounds they hear and acting as scribe. Invite them to copy your writing if they want to. Challenge children to write a simple phrase such as 'Pat is a cat' or 'a hat on a cat'.

Further ideas

• Place the game in a box and write labels and a list of contents for it.
• Look at the interactive picture 'Pet shop' on the CD-ROM and sound out words for the children to find, such as d-o-g and b-a-l-l.

What's in the woods?

CD-ROM resources

Squirrel

Early learning goals

Be confident to try new activities, initiate ideas and speak in a familiar group.

Find out about their environment, and talk about those features they like and dislike.

Setting up

Select a safe area of woodland or trees. In a box place glue sticks, scissors, stapler, grey or brown card strips, card, whole nuts (four per child, with child's initials written on). Check for any nut allergies and choose an alternative if required, such as shells. Find a non-fiction book or a story based on woods. Spread ground sheets on the ground. Draw a simple squirrel outline, cut off the tail and laminate both parts to make a 'Pin the tail on the squirrel' game.

Getting started

- Look at the film clip of the squirrel, noting its features and colours and how it eats and moves about.
- Invite the children to be squirrels, making headbands by sticking ears on the card strips and cutting and stapling to size. Supervise them carefully when using the tools. Suggest that the children take their nuts and hide them ready to find later.
- Move to other areas of the wood. Look at natural and manufactured features, and litter. Play listening and looking games based on what is in the wood, such as I-spy, leaf bingo or silent moving games.
- Ask the children to try and find their buried nuts again. Talk about how hard it is!
- Back indoors, play 'Pin the tail on the squirrel' and finish with a book about woods and compare this with what they have seen. Talk about what the children liked and disliked about the wood.

Let's talk!

Ask, *What does a squirrel look like?* Ask children requiring support, *Where are you going to bury the nuts?* Ask children requiring a challenge, *What could you do next time to help you remember where they are?* Watch to see how the children join in with the different types of activity, which they participate in confidently and for which they need more support. Listen and note which children talk about squirrels and what is in the wood and which suggest a game to play.

Top tip

Remind the children how to play safely in a wood before the visit. Respond sensitively to any children that are scared of woods, perhaps reading a friendly story before the visit.

Differentiation

Point out features of a wood to children needing support. Challenge children to look more closely by asking for three different types of bark pattern or two ways we know people have been there.

Further ideas

- Make a woodland weaving using leaves, fallen bark and natural coloured paper and fabric.

Jungle tent

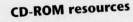

CD-ROM resources

Tiger

Early learning goals

Select and use activities and resources independently.

Show an understanding of the elements of stories, such as main character, sequence of events and openings, and how information can be found in non-fiction texts to answer questions about where, who, why and how.

Setting up

Collect together blankets, sheets and rope with which to make a tent between two trees/fixed points or provide a ready-made tent. Add cushions, blankets and rugs. Select books based on jungle animals such as *Rumble in the Jungle* by Giles Andreae and David Wojtowycz (Orchard Books) and *Jazzy in the Jungle* by Lucy Cousins (Walker Books). Select props such as animal masks and supporting non-fiction material about jungles and animals.

Getting started

- With the children, put up the tent, arranging the rugs and cushions.
- Share both fiction and non-fiction books with the children, talk about jungles and look closely at the photo of the tiger from the CD-ROM and listen to it roar.
- Introduce the props and leave the children to play with them, observing what they do. Return and join in with the play, making the sounds of the animals and introducing new words and vocabulary, based on the books you have read.
- Invite the children to choose a favourite rhyme or story and act it out together. Model good use of language from the texts such as 'I am an elephant and I am going to trumpet really loudly and suck up water and squirt it with a squish!'.
- Leave the children again to develop their play, observing what they do.

Let's talk!

Ask, *What happened at the end of the story/rhyme?* Ask children needing support, *Have you a favourite animal? What sound does it make?* Ask children requiring a challenge, *Can you make a very quiet/loud sound?* During play listen and watch to see which children use the sounds and words from the text and which use their imagination and take on a role. Are the children able to re-tell or act out the texts as a whole or in parts?

Top tip

Place the words of the animals, with accompanying pictures, around the tent in the children's home languages. Invite parents and carers to come in and read a story to the children.

Differentiation

For children needing more support read out a rhyme or story inviting them to act it out with you, taking on a role, which they can copy if they prefer. Challenge children to make up their own story or rhyme. Scribe it for them and ask them to illustrate it, make into a book or hanging and place in the tent.

Further ideas

- Look at the picture 'Tiger in a tropical storm' by Henri Rousseau and compare it with the photo.

On safari

CD-ROM resources

Animal guide

Safari jeep

Tiger

Early learning goals

Observe, find out about and identify features in the place they live and the natural world.

Use language to imagine and recreate roles and experiences.

Setting up

Print off copies of the activity page on the CD-ROM or page 37 in the book and provide colouring and collage materials. Collect a large box for a jeep, binoculars, camera, clothing, maps, soft toys and photos of animals to hide, logs and a torch covered in orange Cellophane. Select books, travel brochures and Internet information on safaris. Provide a shallow paddling pool and water as a watering hole.

Getting started

- With the children, look at the photos of the jeep and the tiger on the CD-ROM and list all the things that you can see, both natural features such as sand, bushes, grass and all the equipment the people have in the jeep. Look at the other sources of information together.
- Show the children the props and invite them to go on safari outside, using the activity sheet as an identification sheet for the animals they see. Leave them to play and observe them, offering help when needed, for example turning the box into a jeep.
- At intervals extend the play by suggesting new ideas, such as one group hides animals for others to spot, or drawing maps showing features and viewing points. Suggest the children decorate animal outlines on the activity sheet for each animal they see.
- Make a pretend campfire with the torch and logs, tell each other about that day's adventure and plan the next day's.

Let's talk!

Ask, *What do you think is happening in the safari jeep photo? How many different things can we see? What equipment will you need to take? How will you travel around? What was your favourite part of going on the safari?* Ask children needing support, *Which animals did you spot?* Ask children requiring a challenge, *What might happen tomorrow?* During play observe which children use the correct words for the equipment and animals. Do they use their new knowledge as they play?

Top tip

Find books, photos, music and film clips of countries visited to go on safari. Compare life there with here.

Differentiation

For children needing more support, go on the safari too, taking on the role of the driver or leader and pointing out things as you travel. Challenge children to find out about camouflage and decorate the animal pictures on the activity sheet so they are difficult to find when hidden outside.

Further ideas

- Make a small world safari park in a sand or builder's tray, grow grass and plants and add a muddy watering hole.

Animal guide

Bear mountain

Early learning goals

Use language such as 'circle' or 'bigger' to describe the shape and size of solids and flat shapes.

Use everyday words to describe position.

Setting up

Make up modelling sand by mixing together six tubs of sand and three tubs of cornflour in an old pan and then adding three tubs of water. Stir over a low heat until thick and leave to cool. Place in a tray with different-sized plastic toy bears and a variety of different shapes and sizes of containers to make mountains. Select the song and photo from the CD-ROM.

Getting started

- Listen to 'The bear went over the mountain' with the children and sing it together adding actions. Look at the photo of the mountains on the CD-ROM and talk about what you can see.
- Show the children the resources in the tray and make model mountains together. Leave the children to explore the sand, listening as they play. Return and sing the song and act it out with the bears in the sand.
- Introduce a game of 'Move the bear', with one child describing where to place the bears among the mountains for another to follow.
- Leave the children to develop their own ideas. Introduce any further resources such as trees, huts and rocks to extend the play.

Let's talk!

Ask, *What shape is the mountain you made? How did you make it? Can you make another mountain that is different? Where is the brown bear?* Support children by asking questions to start with, *Is it next to the tall mountain?* Challenge children to think of two or three ways in which the mountains are different. Listen to the children to find out who uses common words such as *big, bigger, tall, pointy, flat* while playing. Who can explain where the bear is on their own and who understands the vocabulary of position?

Top tip

Find out how to sign the words bear, over, mountain and see and use these actions while singing the song. Encourage children to use the new vocabulary in other situations, such as model making and at home.

Differentiation

Play alongside children needing more support, using the vocabulary as you make mountains and move bears. Challenge children to make a staircase of mountains and hide a different bear behind each one.

Further ideas

- Make meringues and use the mixture to make mountains and other shapes.
- Use salt dough or clay to make model bears.
- Decorate the modelling sand mountains with glass nuggets, shells or tiny flags.

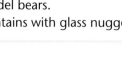

Off to the zoo

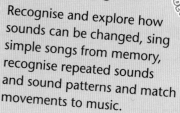
Early learning goals

Recognise and explore how sounds can be changed, sing simple songs from memory, recognise repeated sounds and sound patterns and match movements to music.

Setting up

Select the song from the CD-ROM. Collect together simple instruments and a tape recorder or another way to record the children's song.

Getting started

- Listen to 'Zoo, zoo, who's in the zoo?' with the children and then sing through the song together. Think about the range of noises the animals make and try them out quietly, loudly, quickly, slowly and then in a simple pattern such as loud, loud, soft. Make a mixture of easier and harder sound patterns to copy.
- In a large space move around being the animals, making the pattern of movements with hands and feet. Try making different sounds and types of movement such as clapping, stamping, scuttling sounds with fingers and tapping different parts of the body. Introduce the instruments and invite the children to use these to make sounds as they move.
- Talk about other animals found in the zoo and invite the children to try to make noises and actions for some of these. Share the ideas they have and the sounds they make and add them as verses to the song.
- Make a recording of the song to listen to and join in with. Give the children further opportunities to return to the song and instruments and add new verses.

Let's talk!

Ask, *What noise does your favourite animal in the song make?* Support children by asking, *Can you make this sound? Can you make it quieter than mine?* Ask more able children, *Can you take turns to 'have a conversation' and copy each other's sounds?* Listen to the children as they try out and copy the sounds to find those that can do this independently and accurately. Note who can copy and continue a pattern of sounds and pattern movements.

Top tip

Be aware of the development stages and coordination of individuals in the group when planning the activities. Encourage children to work together to make up new verses helping them share ideas with each other.

Differentiation

Demonstrate some types of sound to children needing more support and ask them to copy yours then try with an instrument of their choice. Challenge children to use materials to make own instruments such as containers, rice, beads, beans, wood, tins, string, clay flower pots and coconut shells to make animal sounds.

Further ideas

- Make paper plate animals adding features with wool, fabric, buttons and paper.
- Read zoo stories such as *Mog at the Zoo* by Helen Nicoll and Jan Pienkowski (Picture Puffin).

Down on the farm

CD-ROM resources

Farm animals

Early learning goals

Use a range of small and large equipment.

Select the tools and techniques they need to shape, assemble and join the materials they are using.

Setting up

Choose a story such as *Pig Gets Lost* by Heather Amery (Usborne Books). Provide different sizes and types of construction toys and materials such as wood, card, boxes, flat small slate pieces and scissors, hole punches, staplers and glue and place them outside. Use some to build a wall around a 'field' on the grass or grass fabric, leave gaps where animals could have escaped and place a range of escaped toy farm animals around the area.

Getting started

- Read the story to the children. Talk about how the animals could have got out and why farmers try to stop the animals escaping.
- Show the children the construction materials and point out the fence with the hole, if the children do not notice it on their own. Explain that the animals have escaped and invite the children to find them and bring them back. Challenge them to make fields, sheds or pens for their animal so they do not escape again.
- Leave the children to come up with their own designs, watching how they approach using the materials and tools. Supervise carefully and offer support if needed. Return and ask the children to talk about their designs.
- Give them the opportunity to choose other animals and try out a different construction toy or materials.

Let's talk!

Ask, *How are you going to keep the animals safe? What are you going to use? What is good about your design?* Ask children requiring support, *Which animal did you choose?* Ask children requiring a challenge, *Is there anything you could change to make it better?* Observe the children as they build to see how they explore and manipulate the materials. Note if they

have a distinct preference for one type of material and if they are still at the playing and exploring stage, prior to constructing for a purpose.

Top tip

Show children how to handle large equipment such as large pieces of wood or boxes safely and explain why this is important. Teach the children the skills needed to build walls and fences then give them plenty of time to practise these.

Differentiation

Start with materials the children are used to, for those needing support. Then introduce the new materials, demonstrating how to use them if appropriate. Challenge children to try and make a gate so the farmer can get into the field.

Further ideas

- Print off the animal cards on the activity sheet on the CD-ROM or page 41 to play dominoes or cut up to make snap and pairs.

Farm animals

Cut out the cards and use them to play dominoes, snap or pairs.

Dinosaurs   Slimy swamp

CD-ROM resources

Swamp

Muddy, murky swamp

In the swamp

Early learning goals

Work as part of a group or class, taking turns and sharing fairly, understanding that there needs to be agreed values and codes of behaviour for groups of people, including adults and children, to work together harmoniously.

Setting up

Place a shallow water or builder's tray outside with stones of different sizes, compost, logs, leaves, twigs, dried grass or hay, small plants and plastic dinosaurs nearby. Provide a container of water, washing-up liquid, pure soap flakes, green paint, bucket or bowl and a whisk. Print the swamp photo from the CD-ROM.

Getting started

- Explore the interactive picture on the CD-ROM together, taking turns to click on the picture. Find out what the children know about dinosaurs. Pass around the photo of the swamp and talk about how some dinosaurs lived in swampy areas. Listen to the rhyme of the baby dinosaur and talk about what he saw around him.
- Take groups of children to the water tray and show them the resources. Ask them to make a home for the baby dinosaur, mixing the ingredients to make green swamp goo.
- Return to the group and look at the home they have created.

Let's talk!

Ask, *Where are the dinosaurs living? What can you find in the picture?* Ask children needing support, *What have you put in the swamp?* Ask children requiring a challenge to develop their ideas, asking *What have the dinosaurs been doing? Which dinosaurs did you use? Where did it go? Did it meet any others? What game did it play?* As the children play, watch and listen to how they interact and collaborate with each other. Note those who can dominate the play, those who are aware of others and can take turns and wait for something and those who are playing alongside others.

Top tip

Observe the group to make sure that some children do not dominate others, suggesting strategies if they do, such as sharing out the resources or taking turns to select a dinosaur. When discussing the swamp games ensure each child is listened to and has a chance to talk, showing you value each child's contribution through relevant comments.

Differentiation

For children needing support, play with two or three children helping them make a swamp together to use with the dinosaurs. Suggest ways of sharing the dinosaurs if appropriate. Challenge children to work together to find out about another environment dinosaurs lived in and set it up to share with the group.

Further ideas

- Read *Harry and the Bucketful of Dinosaurs* by Ian Whybrow (Picture Puffin). Share out a bucket of dinosaur counters and play games with them.

Fantastic fossils

Setting up

ENABLING ENVIRONMENTS

Collect together cold coffee grounds, plain flour, salt, cold coffee, plain flour, and a bowl, cup and spoon for each child ready to make some coffee salt-dough fossils. Select plastic dinosaurs to make effective feet or scale impressions in the dough and leaves and twigs. Obtain some examples of real fossils.

Getting started

- Look at the fossils, compare their shape, size, colour and feel and explain what they are. Look at the footprint photo on the CD-ROM and invite the children to make their own fossil footprint.
- Ask each child to put one cup of cold coffee grounds, two cups of plain flour and one cup of salt in a bowl and mix. Add one cup of cold coffee and mix well to make a soft dough. If too sticky add more flour, if too dry add more coffee. Knead the dough and invite the children to explore it through patting, pulling and poking. Introduce the materials and suggest to the children that they create fossils by pressing things into the dough to make an impression.
- Leave to dry overnight and then bake in a microwave on defrost or in a cool oven until hard and dry. Compare the fossils and find out which items made the print.
- Provide a pictorial copy of the recipe and ingredients for children to make more fossils.

Let's talk!

Ask children needing support, *What colour is your fossil? Can you find some others that are a different colour?* Challenge children by asking, *How are these two fossils similar? How are they different?* Ask more able children to describe the changes between the uncooked and cooked dough. Note how the children explore the properties of the dough and the type of language they use to describe the real and salt-dough fossils.

Top tip

A UNIQUE CHILD

POSITIVE RELATIONSHIPS

Some children may still be putting things in their mouths subconsciously, so remind them at the start of the activity that this mixture is not for tasting! Make up a batch of dough and have fun together exploring its properties. Work with a small group prodding, pulling and poking it and decorating it with natural or manufactured materials.

Differentiation

For children needing more support help them develop an understanding of how to make comparisons, and use their senses, by posing questions such as *Is it soft or hard? Is it large or small?* Challenge children to think of other things that have the same feel as the cooked and uncooked dough.

Further ideas

- Go on a senses walk outside and find things as hard as a dinosaur bone or as rough as their scaly skin.

Dinosaur dig

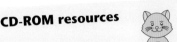
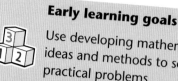

Setting up

In a tray of dry sand or compost place a wide assortment of dried pasta. Alongside place goggles or safety glasses, sieves, scoops, tweezers, small tongs, hand lenses, paintbrushes and collecting trays. Place copies of the activity sheet, printed from the CD-ROM or page 45 in the book, enlarged to A3 alongside the equipment. Have PVA glue, spreaders and a camera available. Find photos or books showing dinosaur skeletons.

Getting started

- Look at the dinosaur skeleton information together and talk about how dinosaur bones have been carefully excavated. Look at the activity sheet together and note how the different bones make up the dinosaurs' bodies.
- Explain that the sand tray is full of 'dinosaur bones' and invite the children to be a dinosaur hunter, or palaeontologist. Ask them to choose a skeleton outline from the activity sheet, put on the goggles and use the equipment to find the bones in the sand to make up their skeleton. Observe as the children search in the sand.
- Give the children the opportunity to glue the 'bones' on the sheet in place or record their skeleton as a photo.

Let's talk!

Ask, *Do you know what a skeleton is? Which bone is the longest/shortest? How many different types of bones have you found? Is your skeleton complete?* Ask children needing support, *What sort of bone are you looking for? Where will you put it? Have you found enough to make the ribs yet?* Challenge children by asking *How many more will you need?* As the children search make note of developing mathematical ideas: counting, matching, sorting, size and shape language, vocabulary relating to addition and subtraction.

Top tip

For those children who find making up the skeletons difficult provide dinosaur outlines that they can decorate with the pasta 'bones'. Check out local museums to see if they have a dinosaur exhibition that families could visit or materials they could bring in to show the children.

Differentiation

Use simpler outlines for children needing support by using correction fluid to hide some of the bones before making copies. Invite children to design their own dinosaur skeleton using bones they excavate. Make photocopies and add to the skeleton outlines for others to try.

Further ideas

- Print dinosaur skeletons on black paper using items such as sticks, straws and cotton reels dipped in white paint.
- Take photos of the activity and use them to make a timeline of how to dig up a dinosaur.

Dinosaur skeletons

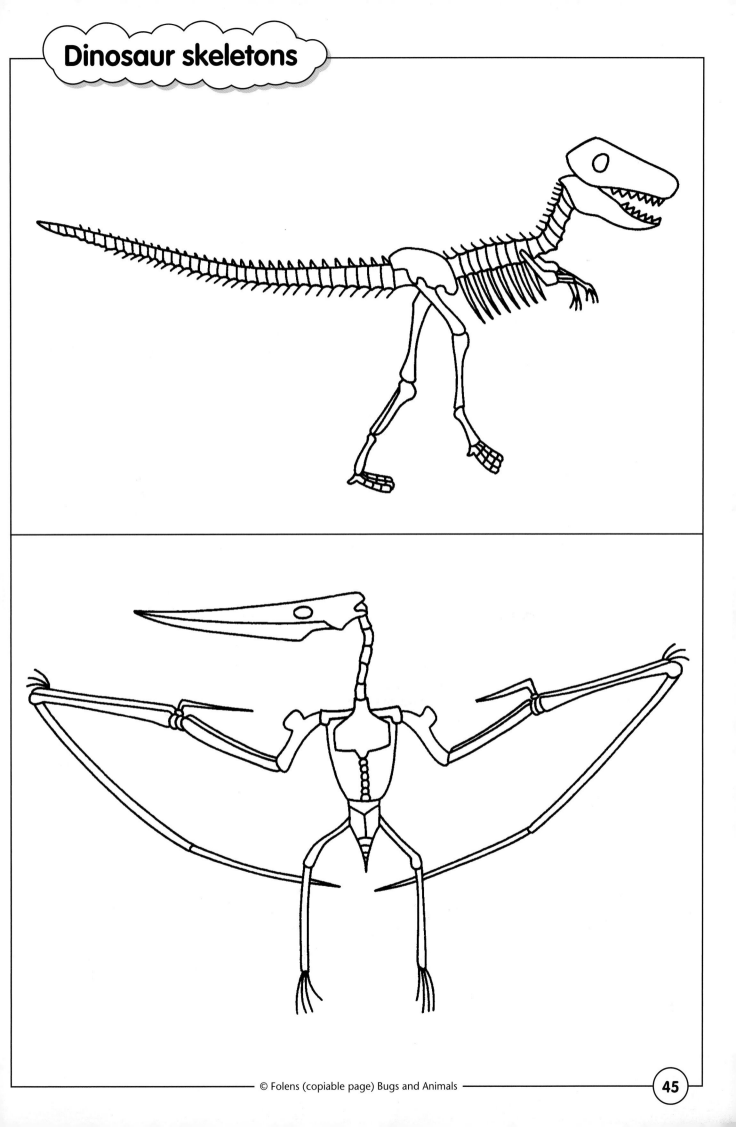

Hungry dinosaurs

CD-ROM resources

Pterosaur in flight

Five hungry pterosaurs

Early learning goals

Listen with enjoyment, and respond to stories, songs and other music, rhymes and poems and make up their own stories, songs, rhymes and poems.

Say and use number names in order in familiar contexts.

Setting up

Set up the CD-ROM ready to view the film clip and listen to the song. Collect together a box of items (decorated with pictures to represent the sea) and include some edible items like bread or fruit, and some inedible such as a book or ball. Place a set of five dinosaur hand puppets inside the box, made from a sock or card.

Getting started

- Watch the film clip together of the pterosaur in flight and then listen to the song on the CD-ROM, joining in as it becomes more familiar and counting down the numbers using fingers to represent each pterosaur.
- Introduce the dinosaur puppets and count them. Explain that they are the hungry dinosaurs from the song and they want something better than fish to eat! Sing through the original song, helping a dinosaur puppet find an item in the box to replace the word fish. Add 'yum' or 'yuk' at the end of the line *catch a … for tea*, depending on what the dinosaur selects.
- Place the box of items and puppets in an accessible place so the children can return to it. Regularly replace the items in the box so the children can make up further songs.

Let's talk!

Ask, *What food do you like to eat? Would you like to eat the same food every day as the dinosaur?* Support children by saying, *Can you sing the song with me? How many dinosaurs are there?* Challenge children by asking, *Do you think this would be good to eat? Why?* Note which children are starting to join in with the repeating refrains. Listen to the children when using the resources independently and see which children know the song by heart, which are making up their own versions based on the original and which are making up totally new songs. Note which children are using number names correctly.

Top tip

Use the box to develop a theme such as healthy snacks or fruit and vegetables. Include items from other cultures and learn the words of the items in a range of languages to reflect the setting, including signed.

Differentiation

Support children by using the recorded song but turn down the volume when the food item is said, so the children can say their item. Invite more able children to think of items for the dinosaur to eat beginning with a certain sound.

Further ideas

- Share dinosaur rhymes or poems such as 'Dinosaur Roar!' by Paul and Henrietta Stickland (Dutton Books).

Dinosaur stomp

CD-ROM resources

Dinosaur footprint

Dinosaur

Early learning goals

LEARNING AND DEVELOPMENT

Move with confidence, imagination and in safety.

Use their imagination in art and design, music, dance, imaginative and role-play and stories.

Setting up

ENABLING ENVIRONMENTS

Select some music with a stomping beat. Collect together empty tissue boxes, paper carrier bags, small boxes and old shoes, together with paint, junk and collage materials, glue, scissors and tape to decorate them. Display the photos of the dinosaur's footprint and the dinosaur from the CD-ROM.

Getting started

- Look at the photo of the dinosaur's footprint and comment on the size compared with the person. Look at the photo of the whole dinosaur model and pay particular attention to the size, shape and features of the feet.
- Go outside and try moving around as large and small dinosaurs, moving in different ways, speeds and directions.
- Invite the children to make a pair of dinosaur feet to wear. Show them the materials and encourage them to choose what they would like to use as the base and decorate it. Supervise them carefully using the tools and materials. Help the children fasten the 'feet' securely to their own.
- In a large space play the music and encourage the children to stomp around, making up their own movements, forwards, backwards and side to side, avoiding bumping into each other. Encourage them to add in arm actions and use their whole body to move like a dinosaur.

Let's talk!

Ask, *What are you going to put on your dinosaur feet? How will you make them stay on?* Support children by asking, *Can you see their claws and the scales?* Challenge children by asking, *What type of dinosaur are you going to be? What movement might it make to the music?* Watch as the children move around to see if they can alter their speed and direction, avoid each other and stop. Can they match their movements to music and come up with imaginative ways of moving of their own?

Top tip

A UNIQUE CHILD

POSITIVE RELATIONSHIPS

Give less confident children time to watch before joining in. Help over enthusiastic children become more aware of others by giving them a focused challenge such as *Can you move along this line?* Share the children's ideas, trying out the ones that they suggest and valuing their efforts.

Differentiation

Support less confident children by suggesting they join up with another child or adult to move around with. Invite more confident children to play follow my leader, taking turns to be a leader and making movements for the others to follow.

Further ideas

- Paint dinosaur footprints outside for the children to run and jump on and over.
- Make dinosaur tabards to wear by decorating a split paper sack or bin bag.

Giant dinosaurs

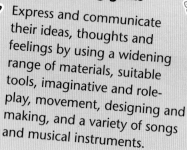

Early learning goals

Express and communicate their ideas, thoughts and feelings by using a widening range of materials, suitable tools, imaginative and role-play, movement, designing and making, and a variety of songs and musical instruments.

Setting up

Select a range of different dinosaur pictures including the one on the CD-ROM. Collect together a range of large tubes, fabric pieces, large rolls of foil, cling film and ribbon, pieces of wood, pebbles and stones, plastic lids and other interesting natural and junk materials and place them in a large space outside. Have a camera available.

Getting started

- Show the children the range of available materials and let them spend time exploring the items. Suggest they try to use the materials to make dinosaurs and show them the photos to provide ideas of outline shapes.
- Look at the different parts of the dinosaurs and think which items could be used for each: for example a dinosaur made on the ground could have eyes made from a ring of fabric or foil with a lid and pebble on top; one peeping out from a tree could be made from fabric and tubes.
- Support the children to think creatively by offering several alternatives, leave them to create their dinosaurs and observe them as they work.
- Return and encourage the children to talk about their creations and share them with each other, then take photos.

Let's talk!

Ask, *What can you do with the fabric? Can you tell me what you have made?* Support children by asking, *Will you use the tubes, fabric or wood for the legs?* Ask other children, *Why did you use this? Why have you placed it there?* Note how the children create their dinosaurs and if they use their own ideas or incorporate or copy those of others. Look at the range of materials and how they have been used, altered and arranged.

Top tip

Give each child time to think about what they want to say about their dinosaurs as some will take time to think their ideas through and become more communicative as interest is shown and positive comments made. Invite a local artist to work with and inspire the children.

Differentiation

Draw outlines on the ground with sand or chalk to inspire children needing more support, or invite them to dress up as dinosaurs. Invite children to work together to make a dinosaur and the landscape showing where it lives.

Further ideas

- Cut out a dinosaur shape from netting and make an outdoor weaving.
- Make giant dinosaurs by covering a row of children with fabric, and adding a head and tail to the front and last ones.